# Fresh & Raw

# Fresh & Raw

eat your way to health and vitality

Contributing Editor
Suzannah Olivier

LORENZ BOOKS

This edition is published by Lorenz Books

Lorenz Books is an imprint of Anness Publishing Ltd
Hermes House, 88–89 Blackfriars Road,
London SE1 8HA
tel. 020 7401 2077; fax 020 7633 9499

www.annesspublishing.com; info@anness.com

© Anness Publishing Ltd 2004

UK agent: The Manning Partnership Ltd, 6 The Old Dairy, Melcombe Road, Bath BA2 3LR;
tel. 01225 478444; fax 01225 478440; sales@manning-partnership.co.uk

UK distributor: Grantham Book Services Ltd, Isaac Newton Way, Alma Park Industrial Estate,
Grantham, Lincs NG31 9SD; tel. 01476 541080; fax 01476 541061; orders@gbs.tbs-ltd.co.uk

North American agent/distributor: National Book Network, 4501 Forbes Boulevard, Suite 200,
Lanham, MD 20706; tel. 301 459 3366; fax 301 429 5746; www.nbnbooks.com

Australian agent/distributor: Pan Macmillan Australia, Level 18, St Martins Tower, 31 Market St,
Sydney, NSW 2000; tel. 1300 135 113; fax 1300 135 103; customer.service@macmillan.com.au

New Zealand agent/distributor: David Bateman Ltd, 30 Tarndale Grove, Off Bush Road,
Albany, Auckland; tel. (09) 415 7664; fax (09) 415 8892

A CIP catalogue record for this book is available from the British Library.

10 9 8 7 6 5 4 3 2 1

## NOTES FOR READERS

Bracketed terms are intended for American readers.

For all recipes, quantities are
given in both metric and imperial
measures and, where appropriate,
measures are also given in standard
cups and spoons Follow one set, but not a
mixture, because they are not interchangeable.

Standard spoon and cup measures are level.

1 tsp = 5ml, 1 tbsp = 15ml, 1 cup = 250ml/8fl oz

Australian standard tablespoons are 20ml. Australian readers should use 3 tsp in place of 1 tbsp for
measuring small quantities of gelatine, flour, salt, etc.

Medium (US large) eggs are used unless otherwise stated.

## SAFETY

The author and publisher can accept no
responsibility for any illness caused by eating
raw food. Please follow the guidelines for food
safety throughout this book and consult your
doctor before commencing a new diet.

• Raw meats or fish and unpasteurized cheeses
or milk should not be eaten if you think you
might be pregnant, or by babies, small children
or the elderly.
• If you have been unwell and your immune
system is not working optimally, it may be best
to avoid raw meat and fish.
• If you are eating raw meat or fish, be very sure
of your supplier to obtain high-quality produce
and make sure the ingredients are super-fresh.
• Raw vegetables and fruit must be washed
to remove any soil residue, which might be
harbouring bacteria.

**Publisher:** Joanna Lorenz

**Editorial Director:** Judith Simons

**Project Editor:** Katy Bevan

**Designer:** Juanita Grout

**Production Controller:** Claire Rae

**Special Recipes:** Becky Johnson

**Special Photography:** Craig Robertson

**Food Styling:** Jenny White

**Additional Recipes:** Pepita Aris, Joanna
Farrow, Becky Johnson, Emi Kazuko, Lucy Knox,
Suzannah Olivier, Keith Richmond, Rena
Salaman, Marlena Spieler, Kate Whiteman

**Additional Photography:** Nicky Dowey,
Gus Filgate, Janine Hosegood, William
Lingwood, Simon Smith

# CONTENTS

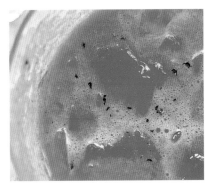

# VITAL FOR HEALTH

If a pill could be invented that gave people healthy skin and extra vitality, and prevented myriad common diseases, it would be in great demand. Yet, in reality, you have only to go to your local greengrocer or supermarket for such a boost. People are becoming increasingly aware of the importance that plenty of fresh and raw foods play in their diet. By incorporating a variety of enzyme-rich vegetables and fruits, and other foods, we can all reap many health benefits.

Although there are some diets that involve eating only fresh fruit, such as grapefruit or bananas, the secret to good health is to do all things in moderation, and that includes eating raw foods. So it is beneficial to include raw foods as part of a healthy diet rather than changing to an all-raw diet.

### RAW HEALTH

Over the last 50 years or so, the science of nutrition has carefully quantified the "nuts and bolts" of foods into proteins, fats, carbohydrates, vitamins and minerals. However, what has remained elusive in scientific terms is the sheer vibrancy of foods. We know that vitamins, minerals and phytonutrients (plant nutrients) have powerful antioxidant values, but it is now thought that the enzyme activity in raw foods is also vital for optimum health.

Enzymes are what make living creatures function. We often think about enzymes as simply having a digestive function – most people are aware that they are necessary for us to digest our food. In fact, enzymes govern every chemical reaction of a living cell, plant or animal.

In evolutionary terms, we started eating cooked food only relatively recently. Cooking certainly makes food taste delicious and enables some elements of food to be more digestible. However, we are not designed to eat a diet that is mainly cooked, or which consists of processed foods, as is typical nowadays. In fact, experiments conducted in the 1930s first demonstrated that if animals were raised on foods that were processed and purified, they developed all the health problems that are common to Westernized societies today, including dental caries, constipation and weakened bones. Whereas vitamin supplements did not completely reverse these adverse effects, raw foods reintroduced into their diets succeeded in returning the animals to full health.

**Below** Colourful salads and green leafy vegetables are great ways to introduce raw foods into your diet.

## ENZYME POWER

There is a school of thought that says that humans have a total "potential" of enzyme activity, and that once this is used up, we degenerate. By obtaining enzymes from our food, we "spare" this enzyme potential and, as a result, live vital and active lives for longer.

Whether this is true or not, it is certainly true that raw foods incorporate enzymes that are specifically designed to aid their digestion and absorption. For example, raw, unpasteurized milk naturally includes the enzyme lactase, which acts on the digestion of the milk sugar, lactose. People who do not produce the milk sugar digesting enzyme, lactase, are unable to digest normal milk but find raw milk much more digestible. Similarly, raw fish, say in the form of the Japanese dish sashimi, includes protease and lipase enzymes, which assist the body to digest the protein and fat in the raw fish.

You can see the activity of enzymes at work in raw foods simply by observing a piece of fruit eventually decomposing in a fruit bowl; the enzymes break down the fruit over time. When food is chewed, the enzymes are "liberated", enabling them to do their work that much faster in the digestive tract, aiding our own digestive enzymes.

Some enzymes are particularly powerful, and it is known that pineapple, rich in the enzyme bromelain, and papaya, rich in the enzyme papain, are powerful protein digesters and are therefore an ideal combination when served with meat. They also "clean up" mucus and dead skin from inside the digestive tract.

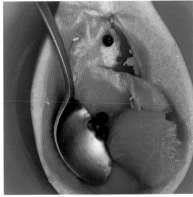

**Above** Raw vegetables and fruit have a fresh and unadulterated taste. Pineapple and papaya have particularly beneficial properties.

### FOOD SAFETY

• Raw meats or fish and unpasteurized cheeses or milk should not be eaten if you think you might be pregnant. The bacteria and other parasites they could contain, such as salmonella, listeria or toxoplasmosis, could have a devastating effect on your developing baby.
• Raw vegetables and fruit must be washed to remove any soil residue which might be harbouring bacteria.

• It is important to remember that one advantage of cooking meat and fish thoroughly is that it kills off any bacteria or other parasites that could be present. For this reason, if you are eating raw meat or fish, be very sure of your supplier in order to obtain high-quality produce that is super-fresh. If you have been unwell and your immune system is not working optimally it may be best to avoid raw meat and fish.

## THE RAW AND THE COOKED

Raw foods are a rich source of vitamins and minerals. When foods are uncooked, valuable nutrients, such as the B vitamins and vitamin C, as well as minerals are preserved, because they are not destroyed by heat or lost into the cooking water. However, some nutrients are made more available to the body when cooked. For example, betacarotene and lycopene (another vital anti-cancer member of the carotene family) are better absorbed from cooked, rather than raw, carrots and tomatoes. What this is probably telling us is that we need a balance of raw versus cooked foods in our diet.

"Raw-fooders" swear by the advantages of eating a totally raw-food diet, but this is probably rather extreme for most people. However, it is true that people who eat nothing but processed and overcooked food will suffer health disadvantages, including sluggishness, weight gain, a poor recovery time from illness and more arthritic conditions.

Most people who eat fairly well still eat only about 20–25 per cent of their diet raw. Pushing this towards 50 per cent could make a significant difference in our health. Although some people may push this to 75 per cent, this is probably not practical for most people on a long-term basis. Indeed, there could be minor upsets due to the digestive system rebelling against the speedy introduction of large amounts of fibre, as the body detoxifies too quickly.

Starting slowly and building up the raw-food habit is the best way forward. It is easy to introduce a little more raw fruit and vegetable matter into your everyday diet, not just with the occasional apple or salad. Get into the habit of "thinking raw" and you will start to enjoy your new regime.

## CHILDREN AND RAW FOODS

It is important to introduce children to raw food early on. Crunching and munching on food is vital for jaw development, and nothing helps this better than regularly snacking on carrot sticks or similar. It is also of great importance for children to become used to the idea that different foods have different textures and to get them used to tasting fresh and interesting foods. All too often children are given bland "kids' foods", which can be fairly insipid and uniform. If we constantly give our children nothing but foods with no "bits" (as is often advertised on the side of yogurt pots), we have only ourselves to blame if they become picky and reject a varied diet. However, children should not be given large quantities of raw foods, as these can be too bulky for their digestive systems.

**Below** Fruits such as pears and oranges that are fresh and raw are alive with enzymes – essential to vitality and health.

# THE RAW-FOOD KITCHEN

It might seem obvious that uncooked food is raw food, but there are also some ways of preparing foods that qualify them as being, in essence, raw, live foods. They may have been prepared in ways to make them more digestible and more interesting to eat, while preserving or enhancing their nutritional value. Some of these methods include dehydrating foods, sprouting beans, grains and pulses, and fermenting, juicing and blending.

### JUICING

Using a blender, juicer or food processor you can make a variety of fruit or vegetable juices at the flick of a switch. Juices are a convenient and delicious way of introducing raw foods into a diet. They make ideal drinks, snacks or breakfasts: after a couple of weeks, a definite and noticeable improvement in health will be noticed by people who drink at least one fresh juice a day. The pasteurized juices found in supermarkets do not provide the same health benefits as those made fresh and raw in your own kitchen.

### DRIED FOODS

Dehydrated foods are an excellent halfway house between raw and cooked foods. Familiar examples are dried fruit, mushrooms and sun-dried tomatoes, now widely available with a hundred uses in the kitchen. Drying foods at

**Above** Consuming raw foods such as beetroot (beet) and other vegetable juices can contribute to improved digestive health; include them as part of a healthy diet.

➤

### CHANGING YOUR DIET
• Eat colourful mixed salads, with the ingredients chopped or grated.
• Cutting out bread and crackers can be awkward, but half-avocados, quarter-peppers and scooped out cucumbers make ideal raw food "boats" for other ingredients as appetizers or a light bite.
• Enjoy vegetable juices, fruity shakes and other raw-food-based drinks.
• A plate of sliced fruit or a fruit salad can be an enjoyable mid-morning treat.

• Fruit puréed and made into a coulis sauce has an intense taste and is excellent served with ripe fruit, such as pear and pineapple or with yogurt. Push the fruit through a fine sieve, or use a blender.
• Dried fruits make delicious snacks or can be used for a winter fruit compote.
• Serve sushi and sashimi for light and healthy main meals.
• Unsalted and unroasted nuts and seeds are nourishing snacks.

• Raw vegetable soups may be heated gently but not cooked.
• Fresh vegetable and fruit crudités with dips make fabulous appetizers, party food or finger food for kids.
• Make dips from sprouted pulses and seeds instead of cooked pulses, and use sprouted pulses, grains and seeds sprinkled on juices or salads.
• Carpaccio and steak tartare are popular and interesting dishes using raw meat or raw oily fish, such as tuna and salmon.

**Above** Making your own yogurt and sprouting your own beans are both cheap and satisfying ways to increase your raw food intake.

home is easy and involves slowly drying the chosen food at between 35–40°C/95–105°F. This is much easier in a special dehydrator, but can be done in a conventional oven set carefully at the correct temperature, with the door slightly ajar to allow steam to escape. It can take 2–10 hours to dehydrate foods depending on the type chosen.

Here are some ideas to try: making your own dried berries, such as blueberries or grapes (for raisins); drying vegetables, such as courgettes (zucchini), onions or mushrooms, to intensify their flavour; and "sun"-drying tomatoes in the oven. Drying citrus peel (from unsprayed fruits only) or herbs, such as mint, sage or young nettle leaves, adds a whole new dimension to flavouring dishes while boosting the nutrient content.

## SPROUTING

If you have never tried freshly made beansprouts, you must taste them to appreciate their delicious nutty flavour. They are extremely versatile and can be used in sandwiches and salads or as snacks. They are also very nutritious: sprouted beans contain vitamins A and B complex, C and E, and the vitamin content can increase by almost 200 per cent when the sprouts begin to turn green on exposure to light, due to the effect of energy-producing chlorophyll.

Beans, pulses and grains contain an array of nutrients that will be needed by the plants as they grow. Beans are not edible when raw, and need to be either cooked or sprouted. When cooked properly, growth inhibitors are deactivated to make them digestible, but beneficial plant enzymes are also destroyed. Sprouting will eliminate these growth enzyme inhibitors, yet fully retain the beneficial plant enzymes.

You can sprout any whole bean, pulse or grain. Favourites are aduki, alfalfa, haricot (navy), lentils, mung, sunflower, cress and wheat sprouts. The smaller beans (legumes) will sprout more successfully than larger ones. Red kidney beans, for example, have a bitter taste and are not easily digested unless they are cooked thoroughly. Always use organic, unsprayed beans from a health food store for sprouting.

You don't need to buy any special equipment for sprouting; you can successfully sprout with just a jam jar, or a colander covered with a cloth, but there are commercial sprouters available. When sprouting beans at home be sure to keep them in a warm, dark place, and rinse them two or three times a day while they grow.

- Phytochemicals such as carotenes (yellow/orange pigments) and anthocyanins (red/purple pigments) are amongst the most potent antioxidants known. Colourful fresh foods, therefore, protect against disease.
- Essential oils, such as those found in citrus peel and fennel, have powerful therapeutic effects on different organs such as the liver or kidneys; bitters found in strong-tasting vegetables, such as Brussels sprouts and broccoli, are known to have cancer-fighting properties.
- Chlorophyll is the green pigment in plants responsible for the miracle of turning light into energy. It is also rich in magnesium – responsible for more than 300 different chemical reactions in our bodies.
- A diet based on fruit and vegetables provides a pH balance supporting the natural alkaline state that the body requires. This is highly protective of urinary tract and bone health.
- A raw diet naturally high in fibre promotes digestive health, protects against cancer and lowers cholesterol.
- You will increase your intake of vitamins and minerals for optimal health.

## CULTURED AND FERMENTED FOODS

Cultures used in yogurts are known to support health by improving the balance of beneficial bacteria in the intestines. This helps both digestive and general immunity. Including live "bio" yogurt on a daily basis is an effective way to improve health. Although commercially made yogurts are made from pasteurized milk, thus eliminating the benefits of raw milk, the lactic acid bacteria that have been used are still truly living as long as the yogurt is made and stored correctly. It is relatively easy to make yogurt at home with a vacuum flask to keep the milk at a constant temperature of 32–40°C/90–105°F, thus ensuring that the beneficial enzymes are not destroyed. However, there are plenty of commercial yogurt kits available. Kefir is a fermented milk product that is not widely available, but as it is a kind of super-yogurt, it is worth buying if you do find it.

Another food that is well known for its health-supporting properties is sauerkraut, which is a famous cornerstone of German cuisine and beneficial when included in the diet occasionally. When the cabbage ferments, the natural sugars convert to lactic acid, promoting more beneficial bacteria in the gut than live yogurt. The Korean version, kimchi, is made in a similar way with garlic, ginger, green onion and radish. These methods of pickling and preserving food developed in cultures where the winters were too cold to grow any fresh produce. Fermentation also renders foods that cause flatulence more digestible, such as members of the cabbage and onion families. However, fermented or pickled foods may cause acid and should therefore be eaten in moderation only as part of a balanced raw- and cooked-food diet.

**Above** Sprouting seeds and beans increases their nutritional value without losing any of the plant enzymes that are good for digestion.

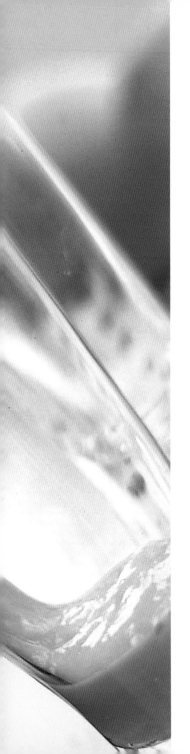

# LIQUID ENERGY

Fresh, raw fruit and vegetables can
be whizzed up in moments to make
energy-packed pick-me-ups that are
as delicious and colourful as they are
healthy and vitalizing. They are
refreshing served as an appetizer or light
meal, and make a perfect late-night
snack, a great wake-up call in the
morning or a nutritious filler at any
time of the day.

Due to its high chlorophyll content, wheatgrass is a powerful detoxifier and cleanser. It is also a rich source of B vitamins, vitamins A, C and E, as well as all the known minerals.

# WHEATGRASS TONIC

Serves 1

### INGREDIENTS

50g/2oz white cabbage

90g/3½oz wheatgrass

| NUTRITIONAL INFORMATION | |
|---|---|
| Per portion | |
| Energy | 32Kcal/131kJ |
| Protein | 3g |
| Carbohydrate | 4g |
| of which sugars | 4g |
| Fat | 0g |
| of which saturates | 0g |
| Cholesterol | 0mg |
| Calcium | 113mg |
| Fibre | 1.1g |
| Sodium | 14mg |

**1** Using a small, sharp knife, roughly shred the cabbage.

**2** Push through a juicer with the wheatgrass. Pour the juice into a small glass and serve immediately.

### COOK'S TIP

Once it is juiced, wheatgrass should be consumed within 15 minutes, preferably on an empty stomach. Wheatgrass juice can have a powerful effect, and some people may feel dizzy or nauseous the first time they drink it. Sip small amounts until your body gets used to it.

### FRESH IDEA – BROCCOLI AND APPLE JUICE

This broccoli juice is combined with sweet and tangy apples to soften its flavour and make a drink that's thoroughly enjoyable. Push 125g/4¼oz broccoli florets and 2 eating apples through a juicer, stir in 15ml/1 tbsp lemon juice to taste and serve with ice. Don't use the tough broccoli stalks, as they provide little juice and don't have as good a flavour as the delicate florets.

Broccoli contains almost as much calcium as milk. Betacarotene, a powerful antioxidant that helps to reduce the risk of cancer and heart disease, is found in broccoli, making this variation a great choice.

This tastebud-tingling combination of sweet grape and sharp apple is a healthy and delicious way to start the day, and will wake up a tired body in place of a caffeine fix.

# SWEET, SHARP SHOCK

**1** Slice some grapes and a sliver or two of apple for the decoration.

**2** Roughly chop the remaining apples. Push through a juicer with the grapes.

**3** Pour over crushed ice, decorate with the sliced fruit and serve immediately. For a longer, more refreshing drink, top up with sparkling mineral water.

### FRESH IDEA – PEA, MELON AND GINGER

Blend ¼ sweet melon, such as Honeydew or Galia, with 200g/7oz sugar snap peas, including their pods. Add a 1cm/½in piece of fresh peeled root ginger to give an edge to this mellow, cooling juice. Keep the melon in the refrigerator so that it's well and truly chilled when you come to blend the juice – you won't need to add ice.

Using sugar snap peas will increase the protein content, and adding melon will make this drink slightly sweeter, but it also provides extra vitamin C, an excellent means of renewing body tissues.

Serves 1

### INGREDIENTS

150g/5oz/1¼ cups red grapes

1 red-skinned eating apple

1 small cooking apple

crushed ice

sparkling mineral water (optional)

| NUTRITIONAL INFORMATION | |
| --- | --- |
| Per portion | |
| Energy | 250Kcal/870kJ |
| Protein | 2g |
| Carbohydrate | 52g |
| of which sugars | 52g |
| Fat | 0g |
| of which saturates | 0g |
| Cholesterol | 0mg |
| Calcium | 28mg |
| Fibre | 53g |
| Sodium | 1mg |

Enjoy this juice as a natural tonic and cleanser. Beetroot has the highest sugar content of any vegetable. Packed with vitamins and minerals, it has a rich but refreshing taste.

# BEETROOT TONIC

Serves 2
### INGREDIENTS

400g/14oz raw beetroot (beets)

2.5cm/1in piece fresh root ginger, peeled

2 large oranges

ice cubes

**1** Trim the beetroot and cut into quarters. Push half the beetroot through a juicer, followed by the ginger and remaining beetroot. Pour into a jug (pitcher).

**2** Squeeze the juice from the orange, by hand or using a citrus juicer, and mix with the beetroot juice.

**3** Pour over ice cubes in two glasses, so the full beauty of the colour can be appreciated. Serve immediately. Don't let the ice cubes melt into the drink or they will dilute it.

### FRESH IDEA – VITAL VEGGIES
For another simple blend, try mixing 250g/9oz carrots and 3 tomatoes pepped up with 1 red or green chilli and the juice of an orange. Push the carrots through a juicer, then follow with the tomatoes and chilli. Add orange juice and stir well to mix. Serve with crushed ice. If you prefer a less fiery juice, remove the seeds and pith from the chilli before juicing.

Tomatoes and carrots are rich in the antioxidant betacarotene, reputed to fight cancer, and contain a good supply of vitamins A, C and E, all of which are essential for health.

### NUTRITIONAL INFORMATION

| Per portion | |
|---|---|
| Energy | 148Kcal/634kJ |
| Protein | 6g |
| Carbohydrate | 32g |
| of which sugars | 30g |
| Fat | 1g |
| of which saturates | 0g |
| Cholesterol | 0mg |
| Calcium | 132mg |
| Fibre | 7.1g |
| Sodium | 141mg |

A tangy, fruity blend of soft, ripe mango with yogurt, sharp, zesty lime and lemon juice makes a wonderfully thick, cooling drink that's refreshing and packed with energy.

# MANGO AND LIME LASSI

**1** Peel the mango and cut the flesh from the stone (pit). Put the flesh into a food processor or blender and add the lime rind and juice.

**2** Add the lemon juice, sugar and natural yogurt. Whizz until completely smooth, scraping down the sides once or twice. Stir a little mineral water into the mixture to thin it down for drinking.

**3** Serve immediately, with half a lime on the side of each glass so that more juice can be squeezed in if desired.

### FRESH IDEA – TOFU SMOOTHIE

For a dairy-free version, blend 150g/5oz natural tofu with the freshly squeezed juice of 2 oranges, 15ml/ 1 tbsp lemon and 20–25ml/4–5 tsp fragrant honey. Whizz the ingredients in a blender or food processor until very smooth and creamy, and serve in a tall glass with some pared orange rind to decorate.

Try to find silken tofu, as it has a satiny texture that

blends particularly well. Bone-building calcium is found in tofu along with the positive benefits of isoflavones, which help to fight against some of the more unpleasant symptoms of the menopause.

Serves 2

### INGREDIENTS

1 mango

finely grated rind and juice of 1 lime

15ml/1 tbsp lemon juice

5–10ml/1–2 tsp caster (superfine) sugar

100ml/3½fl oz/scant ½cup natural (plain) yogurt

mineral water

1 extra lime, halved, to serve

### NUTRITIONAL INFORMATION

| Per portion | |
|---|---|
| Energy | 103Kcal/438kJ |
| Protein | 3g |
| Carbohydrate | 20g |
| of which sugars | 20g |
| Fat | 2g |
| of which saturates | 1g |
| Cholesterol | 6mg |
| Calcium | 110mg |
| Fibre | 2g |
| Sodium | 42mg |

Enjoy the perfect option for a healthy and nourishing breakfast in bed without the crumbs. Apricot, ginger and muesli are perfect partners in this divine drink.

# SMOOTH START

Serves 2

## INGREDIENTS

1 piece preserved stem ginger, plus 30ml/2 tbsp syrup from the ginger jar

50g/2oz/¼ cup ready-to-eat dried apricots, halved or quartered

40g/1½ oz/scant ½ cup natural muesli (granola)

about 200ml/7fl oz/scant 1 cup semi-skimmed (low-fat) milk

**1** Chop the preserved ginger and put it in a blender or food processor with the syrup, apricots, muesli and milk.

**2** Process until smooth, adding more milk if necessary. Serve in wide glasses.

**COOK'S TIP** The drink can be covered and chilled overnight, but you may need to add more milk in the morning if it has thickened up.

## FRESH IDEA – BIG BREAKFAST SMOOTHIE

For an alternative, peel a banana and break it into short lengths. Skin a mango, slice the flesh off the stone (pit) and put it in a food processor or blender with the banana. Squeeze the juice from an orange and add to the food processor or blender with 30ml/2 tbsp bran, 15ml/1 tbsp sesame seeds and 10–15ml/2–3 tsp honey. Whizz until the mixture is smooth and creamy, then pour into two glasses and serve.

Bananas and sesame seeds provide the perfect fuel in the form of slow-release carbohydrate that will keep you going all morning, while fresh orange juice and sweet mango will set your taste buds tingling.

## NUTRITIONAL INFORMATION

| Per portion | |
| --- | --- |
| Energy | 182Kcal/774kJ |
| Protein | 7g |
| Carbohydrate | 33g |
| of which sugars | 23g |
| Fat | 3g |
| of which saturates | 1g |
| Cholesterol | 6mg |
| Calcium | 149mg |
| Fibre | 3.1g |
| Sodium | 76mg |

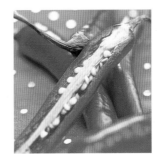

# VEG OUT

One of life's great pleasures is selecting and eating fresh raw vegetables, whether straight from the garden, chosen from a mouthwatering display in a farmer's market or from a precious store in the middle of winter. Eating them raw rather than cooked means that all the beneficial nutrients, vitamins and minerals will be available to your body and not lost in the cooking water.

Papaya contains the potent protein-digesting enzyme papain, which can help to restore a healthy bacterial balance in the digestive tract. It is also rich in betacarotene and vitamin C.

# GREEN PAPAYA SALAD

Serves 4

**INGREDIENTS**

1 green papaya

4 garlic cloves, coarsely chopped

15ml/1 tbsp chopped shallots

3–4 fresh red chillies, seeded and sliced

2.5ml/½ tsp salt

2–3 snake beans or 6 green beans, cut into 2cm/¾in lengths

2 tomatoes, cut into thin wedges

45ml/3 tbsp Thai fish sauce

15ml/1 tbsp caster (superfine) sugar

juice of 1 lime

30ml/2 tbsp crushed roasted peanuts

sliced fresh red chillies, to garnish

**NUTRITIONAL INFORMATION**

Per portion
Energy          82Kcal/345kJ
Protein                    3g
Carbohydrate               8g
  of which sugars          6g
Fat                        4g
  of which saturates       1g
Cholesterol             23mg
Calcium                  0mg
Fibre                      2g
Sodium                 750mg

**1** Cut the papaya in half lengthways. Scrape out the seeds with a spoon and discard, then peel, using a swivel vegetable peeler or a small sharp knife. Shred the flesh finely in a food processor or using a grater.

**2** Put the garlic, shallots, red chillies and salt in a large mortar and grind to a paste with a pestle. Add the shredded papaya, a small amount at a time, pounding with the pestle until it becomes slightly limp and soft.

**3** Add the sliced snake or green beans and wedges of tomato to the mortar and crush them lightly with the pestle until they are incorporated.

**4** Season the mixture with the fish sauce, sugar and lime juice. Transfer the salad to a serving dish and sprinkle with the crushed roasted peanuts. Garnish with the sliced red chillies and serve the salad immediately.

**COOK'S TIP** Unlike the deliciously sweet ripe papaya, fresh-tasting green papaya is used like a vegetable. However, if you can't get hold of green papaya, substitute with finely grated carrots, cucumber, very thinly sliced white cabbage or even a tart, crisp green apple. Snake beans are also known as long beans, as they can be up to 35cm/14in long. They are available in most Asian stores, or you can substitute other green beans.

Serve this crunchy salad, bursting with the flavours of fresh herbs, for lunch or a light supper. Accompanied by crème fraîche or yogurt cheese, it makes a balanced and healthy meal.

# WILD GREENS WITH OLIVES AND HERBS

## NUTRITIONAL INFORMATION

Per portion
| | |
|---|---|
| Energy | 152Kcal/632kJ |
| Protein | 3g |
| Carbohydrate | 11g |
| of which sugars | 10g |
| Fat | 11g |
| of which saturates | 2g |
| Cholesterol | 0mg |
| Calcium | 87mg |
| Fibre | 4.5g |
| Sodium | 356mg |

Serves 4

### INGREDIENTS

1 large bunch wild rocket (arugula), about 115g/4oz

1 large bunch mixed salad leaves

¼ white cabbage, thinly sliced

1 cucumber, sliced

1 small red onion, chopped

2–3 garlic cloves, chopped

3–5 tomatoes, cut into wedges

1 green (bell) pepper, seeded and sliced

2–3 fresh mint sprigs, sliced or torn

15–30ml/1–2 tbsp chopped fresh parsley and/or tarragon or dill

pinch of dried oregano or thyme

45ml/3 tbsp extra virgin olive oil

juice of ½ lemon

15ml/1 tbsp red wine vinegar

15–20 black olives

salt and black pepper

**1** Put the rocket into a large salad bowl. Add the mixed salad leaves, white cabbage, cucumber, onion and garlic. Toss gently with your fingers to combine.

**2** Arrange the tomatoes, pepper and fresh herbs on top of the greens and vegetables. Sprinkle over the dried herbs and season. Drizzle over the oil, lemon juice and vinegar, stud with the olives and serve.

**COOK'S TIP** Try to find mixed salad leaves that include varieties such as lamb's lettuce, purslane and mizuna. To make yogurt cheese, mash a little feta into natural (plain) yogurt. Alternatively, serve with cottage or cream cheese flavoured with black pepper and herbs.

### FRESH IDEA – WILD ROCKET SALAD

Try this combination for a sharp-edged salad. It is important to balance the bitterness of the rocket and the sweetness of the cos lettuce, and the best way to find out if the balance is right is by taste.

Mix two large handfuls of rocket leaves with the sliced hearts of two cos or romaine lettuces, and some fresh dill and chopped parsley. Serve with a dressing made from olive oil and lemon juice.

Carrots are rich in betacarotene, which is good for the immune system as well as skin and eye health. They also contain an easily absorbed source of calcium.

# MATCHSTICK CARROTS

**1** Cut the carrots into thin matchsticks, 5cm/2in long. Put the carrots and salt into a mixing bowl and mix well with your hands. Leave for 25 minutes, and then rinse the wilted carrot in cold water and drain.

**2** In another bowl, mix together the marinade ingredients. Add the carrots, and leave them to marinate for 3 hours.

**3** Chop the sesame seeds with a large, sharp knife on a large chopping board. Place the carrots in a bowl, sprinkle with the sesame seeds and serve cold.

### FRESH IDEA – RED COLESLAW

Thinly slice half a red cabbage, and mix in a bowl with 1 chopped red (bell) pepper and half a red onion. Dissolve 60ml/4 tbsp sugar in 60ml/4 tbsp warmed wine or cider vinegar and then pour over the vegetables. Leave to cool slightly. If you wish, combine some yogurt and mayonnaise, then mix into the cabbage mixture. Season to taste with curry powder, salt and ground black pepper, then mix in 2–3 handfuls of raisins. Chill for at least 2 hours. Just before serving, drain off any excess liquid and briefly stir the slaw.

Serves 4

### INGREDIENTS

2 large carrots, peeled

5ml/1 tsp salt

30ml/2 tbsp sesame seeds

### For the sweet vinegar marinade

75ml/5 tbsp rice vinegar

30ml/2 tbsp shoyu (use the pale awakuchi soy sauce if available)

45ml/3 tbsp mirin

### NUTRITIONAL INFORMATION

Per portion
| | |
|---|---|
| Energy | 86Kcal/358kJ |
| Protein | 2g |
| Carbohydrate | 7g |
| of which sugars | 6g |
| Fat | 4g |
| of which saturates | 1g |
| Cholesterol | 0mg |
| Calcium | 65mg |
| Fibre | 2.3g |
| Sodium | 514mg |

This dish contains acids that keep the gut healthy, and essential minerals and trace elements. Sauerkraut is a traditional source of vitamin C in climates where fresh winter vegetables are scarce.

# SAUERKRAUT

**Serves 4**

### INGREDIENTS

1 cabbage, red, white or green, coarsely grated – reserve some of the large outer leaves whole

15ml/1 tbsp dried juniper berries, crushed in a pestle and mortar or spice grinder or 15ml/1 tbsp dill or caraway seeds

10g/¼oz dried and finely shredded hijiki or arame seaweed

30ml/2 tbsp mustard seed

**1** Place all the ingredients in a large stainless steel or ceramic pan or bowl, and pound with the end of a wooden rolling pin or a pestle until you have a juicy mass.

**2** Cover with the reserved cabbage leaves and a plate and press down. Weigh down the plate with heavy weights, such as full cans, to compound the mixture, and then cover the whole container with a cloth, which will allow the air to circulate.

**3** Leave for 5–10 days, depending on the room temperature, in which time the cabbage will ferment to a fresh-smelling sauerkraut. Don't panic when the cabbage smells strongly on day two or three as this phase will soon pass.

**4** Transfer to glass storage jars and keep in the refrigerator for up to 3 weeks.

**COOK'S TIPS** Sauerkraut can be made with grated carrot or beetroot (beets), mixed with or instead of the cabbage. Hijiki seaweed is a black marine algae that grows up to 1m/3ft long all around the Japanese coast. It is full of vitamins and minerals, including calcium and fibre, and contains no fat. It can be purchased dried in packets from most Asian food stores and some health food stores.

## NUTRITIONAL INFORMATION

Per portion
| | |
|---|---|
| Energy | 34Kcal/144kJ |
| Protein | 4g |
| Carbohydrate | 5g |
| of which sugars | 5g |
| Fat | 2g |
| of which saturates | 0g |
| Cholesterol | 0mg |
| Calcium | 122mg |
| Fibre | 4.2g |
| Sodium | 87mg |

This Middle Eastern recipe gives healthy pickled raw vegetables a hot and spicy lift. The dish takes at least 5 hours to pickle, so start preparations in advance.

# INSTANT PICKLES

**1** Toss the cauliflower, carrots, celery, cabbage, beans, garlic, chillies, ginger and pepper with a little salt and leave to stand in a colander for 4 hours.

**2** Transfer the salted vegetables to a bowl and add the turmeric, vinegar, oil and lemon juice. Add sugar to taste. Toss to combine, then add enough water to balance the flavours.

**3** Cover and chill for at least 1 hour, or until ready to serve. This pickle can be stored in the refrigerator for up to 2 weeks.

### FRESH IDEA – PICKLED BROCCOLI STEMS

You may be surprised at how tasty the fibrous stems of broccoli can be, and the extra betacarotene is a bonus. Marinate 3 stems with 2 halved and seeded cucumbers. For the marinade mix 200ml/7fl oz/scant 1 cup miso, 15ml/1 tbsp sake and 1 crushed garlic clove in a deep plastic or metal container with a lid. Lay some broccoli stems and some of the cucumber in the container and push in half the miso mix. Spread more of the miso mix over the top of the broccoli and repeat this process. Cover and refrigerate for 1–5 days.

Serves 12

### INGREDIENTS

½ cauliflower head, cut into florets

2 carrots, sliced

2 celery sticks, thinly sliced

¼–½ cabbage, thinly sliced

115g/4oz runner (green) beans, cut into bitesize pieces

6 garlic cloves, sliced

1–4 fresh chillies, whole or sliced

30–45ml/2–3 tbsp sliced fresh root ginger

1 red (bell) pepper, sliced

2.5ml/½ tsp turmeric

105ml/7 tbsp white wine vinegar

60–90ml/4–6 tbsp olive oil

juice of 2 lemons

15–30ml/1–2 tbsp sugar

salt

### NUTRITIONAL INFORMATION

Per portion
| | |
|---|---|
| Energy | 75Kcal/312kJ |
| Protein | 1g |
| Carbohydrate | 6g |
| of which sugars | 6g |
| Fat | 5g |
| of which saturates | 1g |
| Cholesterol | 0mg |
| Calcium | 25mg |
| Fibre | 1.6g |
| Sodium | 9mg |

# CHILL

Raw, chilled, really fresh beef and fish pack a taste and health punch that is out of this world, allowing us to benefit from the flavour and goodness that are otherwise lost in cooking. The texture of uncooked meat and fish has long been appreciated in different cultures where the freshest produce is available locally – these days we can all enjoy it.

Uncooked, hand-minced steak is seasoned to taste and served here with a raw egg yolk. The steak can be served with a selection of finely chopped vegetables to enhance the flavour.

# STEAK TARTARE

Serves 4

### INGREDIENTS

450g/1lb fillet steak (beef tenderloin)

1 small onion, finely chopped

30ml/2 tbsp chopped fresh parsley

4 egg yolks

salt and black pepper

**1** Finely mince (grind) the steak by chopping it using a pair of very sharp knives. Hold one knife in each hand and use a chopping action. Use the flat of the blades to bring in the meat from the sides so it is evenly chopped.

**2** Stir in the onion, parsley, salt and black pepper.

**3** Arrange the steak in mounds on four chilled plates. Make a hollow in the middle of each. Place an egg yolk in each hollow and serve.

**COOK'S TIPS** It is vital that both the meat and eggs used in this recipe are perfectly fresh and bought from reliable suppliers. The meat must be minced at home to avoid any risk of cross-contamination.

Keep cooking equipment scrupulously clean, especially chopping boards. Wooden boards are traditionally used, but the surface can become scored and will then harbour bacteria. Plastic chopping boards can be thoroughly washed in a dishwasher and so are easier to keep clean.

Raw meat should be stored on the coldest shelf of the refrigerator, either in its packaging or in a covered dish, and well away from any other meat or cooked foods.

### NUTRITIONAL INFORMATION

| Per portion | |
|---|---|
| Energy | 224Kcal/936kJ |
| Protein | 27g |
| Carbohydrate | 1g |
| of which sugars | 1g |
| Fat | 12g |
| of which saturates | 5g |
| Cholesterol | 270mg |
| Calcium | 35mg |
| Fibre | 0.3g |
| Sodium | 158mg |

The taste and texture of good raw fillet beef is something to be savoured. The combination of ginger, garlic and soy sauce will add a tang to the final delicious melt-in-the-mouth experience.

# CARPACCIO OF BEEF

Serves 6–8

### INGREDIENTS

250ml/8fl oz/1 cup soy sauce

175ml/6fl oz/¾ cup vegetable oil

50ml/2fl oz/¼ cup ground nut (peanut) oil

4 garlic cloves, crushed

2.5cm/1in fresh root ginger

450g/1lb fillet steak (beef tenderloin)

1 chunk Gruyere cheese

vinaigrette, to serve

**1** Combine the soy sauce, oils and garlic. Peel and chop the ginger and add to the bowl.

**2** Marinate the beef in the mixture for at least 4–5 hours and preferably overnight.

**3** About 30–45 minutes before you are ready to serve, put the steak in the freezer to firm up.

**4** Slice the steak very thinly. Crumble or shave some of the cheese on top, drizzle with the vinaigrette and serve on a very cold plate.

### FRESH IDEA – TUNA CARPACCIO

If you are keeping the saturated fats down, fresh tuna is an excellent alternative to the steak in this recipe. Roll the tuna tightly in clear film and place in the freezer for 4 hours. Unwrap, slice into very thin rounds and marinate for a maximum of 2–3 hours. Tuna is high in omega 3 fatty acids, which help to protect against

heart disease. Fish oils are also beneficial to people who suffer from rheumatoid arthritis, as they are less inflammatory in the body than animal fats. Fish oils in the diet make a modest improvement to joint pain.

| NUTRITIONAL INFORMATION | |
| --- | --- |
| Per portion | |
| Energy | 375Kcal/1548kJ |
| Protein | 16g |
| Carbohydrate | 3g |
| of which sugars | 0g |
| Fat | 33g |
| of which saturates | 6g |
| Cholesterol | 39mg |
| Calcium | 56mg |
| Fibre | 0.1g |
| Sodium | 1846mg |

In this attractive salad, the marinade of lemon and dashi-konbu "cooks" the salmon, which is then served with avocado, almonds and salad leaves and accompanied by a miso mayonnaise.

# MARINATED SALMON WITH AVOCADO

**1** Cut the first salmon fillet in half crossways at the tail end where the fillet is not wider than 4cm/1½in. Next, cut the wider part in half lengthways. This means that the two fillets will be cut into four pieces.

**2** Put the lemon juice and two of the dashi-konbu pieces into a wide, shallow plastic container. Lay the salmon fillets in the base and add the rest of the dashi-konbu. Marinate for about 15 minutes, then turn once and leave for a further 15 minutes. The salmon should change to a pink "cooked" colour.

**3** Remove the salmon from the marinade and wipe with kitchen paper. Reserve the marinade. Holding a sharp knife at an angle, cut the salmon into 5mm/¼in thick slices against the grain. Halve the avocado, remove the avocado stone (pit) and skin, then carefully slice to the same thickness as the salmon.

**4** Mix the miso mayonnaise ingredients in a small bowl. Spread about 5ml/1 tsp on to the back of each of the shiso leaves, then mix the remainder with 15ml/1 tbsp of the remaining marinade. Arrange the salad on plates and top with the avocado, salmon, shiso leaves and almonds. Drizzle over the remaining miso mayonnaise.

**COOK'S TIP** Shiso leaves, dashi-konbu and miso are all generally available from Asian food stores.

Serves 4

**INGREDIENTS**

250g/9oz very fresh salmon tail, skinned and filleted

juice of 1 lemon

10cm/4in dashi-konbu, wiped with a damp cloth and cut into 4 strips

1 ripe avocado

4 shiso leaves, stalks removed and cut in half lengthways

about 115g/4oz mixed leaves, such as lamb's lettuce, frisée or rocket (arugula)

45ml/3 tbsp flaked (sliced) almonds

**For the miso mayonnaise**

90ml/6 tbsp good quality mayonnaise

15ml/1 tbsp shiro miso

ground black pepper

NUTRITIONAL INFORMATION

Per portion
Energy      418Kcal/1729kJ
Protein                    17g
Carbohydrate                3g
  of which sugars           1g
Fat                        38g
  of which saturates        6g
Cholesterol              48mg
Calcium                  68mg
Fibre                     3.1g
Sodium                  294mg

This quickest of dishes is also one of the most delicious and nutritious. The savoury shoyu and peppery horseradish wasabi give it an authentic Japanese twist.

# CUBED AND MARINATED TUNA

Serves 4

### INGREDIENTS

400g/14oz very fresh tuna, skinned

1 carton mustard and cress (optional)

20ml/4 tsp wasabi paste from a tube, or the same amount of wasabi powder mixed with 10ml/2 tsp water

60ml/4 tbsp shoyu

8 spring onions (scallions), green part only, finely chopped

4 shiso leaves, cut into thin slivers lengthways

**1** Cut the tuna into 2cm/¾in cubes. If using mustard and cress, tie into pretty bunches or arrange as a bed in four small serving bowls or plates.

**2** Just 5–10 minutes before serving, blend the wasabi paste with the shoyu in a bowl, then add the tuna and spring onions.

**3** Mix well and leave to marinate for 5 minutes.

**4** Divide among the bowls and add a few slivers of shiso leaves on top. Serve immediately.

### FRESH IDEA – CEVICHE

Cut 675g/1½lb halibut, turbot, sea bass or salmon fillets into strips. Lay them in a shallow dish and pour over the juice of 3 limes, turning to coat them in the juice. Cover with clear film (plastic wrap) and leave for 1 hour. Season the fish with salt, and scatter over 1–2 fresh red chillies, seeded and very finely chopped. Drizzle with 15ml/1 tbsp olive oil. Toss the fish in the mixture, then replace the cover. Leave to marinate in the refrigerator for 15–30 minutes more. The fish must be absolutely fresh for this recipe.

NUTRITIONAL INFORMATION

Per portion
Energy          154Kcal/650kJ
Protein                    26g
Carbohydrate                2g
  of which sugars           1g
Fat                         5g
  of which saturates        1g
Cholesterol              28mg
Calcium                  36mg
Fibre                    0.7g
Sodium                  908mg

The fine flavour of turbot is set off to perfection by a piquant dressing in this simple sashimi salad. The fish changes colour and texture as it is plunged into the icy water.

# TURBOT SALAD WITH WASABI

**1** First make the dressing. Roughly tear the rocket leaves and process with the cucumber and rice vinegar in a food processor or blender. Pour into a small bowl and add the olive oil and salt. Check the seasoning and add more salt, if required. Chill until needed.

**2** Chill the serving plates while you prepare the fish, if you like.

**3** Prepare a bowl of cold water with a few ice cubes. Cut the turbot fillet in half lengthways, then cut into 5mm/¼in thick slices crossways. Plunge these into the ice-cold water as you slice. After 2 minutes or so, they will start to curl and become firm. Take out and drain on kitchen paper.

**4** In a large bowl, mix the fish, salad leaves and radishes. Mix the wasabi into the dressing and toss well with the salad. Serve immediately.

**COOK'S TIP** Wasabi is a pungent Japanese condiment made from the mountain hollyhock. It is sometimes introduced as the Japanese equivalent of horseradish, although the two are not related. When grated, fresh wasabi reveals a vivid green flesh, but the root is most commonly found in its powdered or paste forms, now widely available all over the world.

Serves 4

### INGREDIENTS

ice cubes

400g/14oz very fresh thick turbot, skinned and filleted

300g/11oz mixed salad leaves

8 radishes, thinly sliced

#### For the wasabi dressing

25g/1oz rocket (arugula) leaves

50g/2oz cucumber, chopped

90ml/6 tbsp rice vinegar (use brown if available)

75ml/5 tbsp olive oil

about 5ml/1 tsp salt

15ml/1 tbsp wasabi paste from a tube, or the same amount of wasabi powder mixed with 7.5ml/1½ tsp water

| NUTRITIONAL INFORMATION | |
|---|---|
| Per portion | |
| Energy | 240Kcal/1000kJ |
| Protein | 19g |
| Carbohydrate | 2g |
| of which sugars | 2g |
| Fat | 17g |
| of which saturates | 3g |
| Cholesterol | 0mg |
| Calcium | 82mg |
| Fibre | 1.2g |
| Sodium | 565mg |

Marinating is particularly associated with anchovies, which tend to lose their freshness very quickly. This is one of the simplest ways to prepare and preserve these tiny fish.

# MARINATED ANCHOVIES

**Serves 4**

### INGREDIENTS

225g/8oz fresh anchovies, heads and tails removed, cleaned and gutted

juice of 3 lemons

30ml/2 tbsp extra virgin olive oil

2 garlic cloves, finely chopped

15ml/1 tbsp chopped fresh parsley

flaked sea salt

### NUTRITIONAL INFORMATION

| Per portion | |
| --- | --- |
| Energy | 147Kcal/613kJ |
| Protein | 12g |
| Carbohydrate | 1g |
| of which sugars | 1g |
| Fat | 11g |
| of which saturates | 2g |
| Cholesterol | 0mg |
| Calcium | 52mg |
| Fibre | 0.1g |
| Sodium | 167mg |

**1** Turn the anchovies on to their bellies, and press down with your thumb. Using the tip of a small, sharp knife, carefully remove the backbones from the flattened fish and arrange the anchovies skin side down in a single layer on a large plate.

**2** Squeeze two-thirds of the lemon juice over the fish and sprinkle them with a little salt. Cover and leave to stand for 12–24 hours, basting occasionally with the juices, until the flesh is white and no longer translucent.

**3** Transfer the anchovies to a serving plate and drizzle with the olive oil and the remaining lemon juice. Scatter over the chopped garlic and parsley, then cover with clear film (plastic wrap) and chill until ready to serve.

**COOK'S TIP** Not many people are aware that anchovies are not small sardines or pilchards but tiny fish with their own distinctive flavour. In Mediterranean

countries, they are often enjoyed fresh, rather than canned, in this simple marinade. Anchovies are so rich in omega 3 fatty acids that they are often used as the source for food supplements.

# SEED, NUT AND SPROUT

Seeds, nuts and sprouts are the power-houses of raw food, packed with vitamins and minerals as well as flavour. There is almost 30 per cent more B vitamins and 60 per cent more vitamin C in a sprout than in the original seed, pulse or grain. Nuts are rich in essential fatty acids, protein and the antioxidant vitamin E, which is associated with a lower risk of heart disease, stroke and certain cancers.

This creamy-textured "cheese" provides a delicious and easily digestible way of eating seeds and accessing all their valuable nutrients. Serve in curls of lettuce or chicory leaves.

# THREE-SEED CHEESE

**1** To sprout the seeds, rinse them in cold water and place them in a large jar. Cover with spring water and leave to soak for 5 hours in a warm place but keep out of direct sunlight.

**2** Drain, then replace in the jar and cover with a cloth for a further 24 hours, or until just sprouting. The sprouts should be eaten immediately or placed in plastic bags in the refrigerator and eaten within 2 days.

**3** Blend the sprouts with a little spring water in a food processor to a smooth, thick consistency. Place in a clean dishtowel or muslin bag and hang up to drip-dry for a few hours.

**COOK'S TIP** The "cheese" can be kept in a glass storage jar in the refrigerator for up to 2 days, but it is better eaten before chilling on the day it is made.

## FRESH IDEA – SEED CRISPS
Try adding fresh herbs or seaweed to the blend for extra flavour. Place spoonfuls of the freshly made mix on to sheets of baking parchment and allow it to dry out to make little crisps. These can be kept in an airtight box for up to a week. Use as an accompaniment to salads or raw soups. Seaweed gives an important boost to this "cheese", as the iodine it contains helps to regulate the metabolism.

Serves 2
### INGREDIENTS
30ml/2 tbsp sunflower seeds

30ml/2 tbsp pumpkin seeds

15ml/1 tbsp sesame seeds

### NUTRITIONAL INFORMATION

| Per portion | |
| --- | --- |
| Energy | 16Kcal/66kJ |
| Protein | 1g |
| Carbohydrate | 2g |
| of which sugars | 1g |
| Fat | 0g |
| of which saturates | 0g |
| Cholesterol | 0mg |
| Calcium | 10mg |
| Fibre | 0.8g |
| Sodium | 0.3mg |

Grinding nuts releases their oils to form a thick paste with a fantastic flavour and a smooth, buttery texture. Enjoy with salads and sprouts, or on slices of pear, crunchy apple or celery.

# ALMOND AND CASHEW NUT BUTTER

Serves 2

### INGREDIENTS

50g/2oz/½ cup almonds

100g/3½oz/scant 1 cup cashew nuts

**NUTRITIONAL INFORMATION**

Per portion
Energy      440Kcal/1821kJ
Protein                       14g
Carbohydrate              11g
  of which sugars          3g
Fat                              38g
  of which saturates      6g
Cholesterol                0mg
Calcium                    76mg
Fibre                         3.5g
Sodium                      1mg

**1** Process the almonds and cashews in a blender until they release their oils and form a thick buttery paste. Nut butter will keep for up to 1 week in a jar in the refrigerator.

**COOK'S TIP** Try using walnuts or pecans instead of the almonds. Hazelnuts and almonds have a lower fat content than cashews, walnuts and pecans, so need to be mixed with cashews or peanuts to get a smooth, buttery texture. Walnuts on their own are quite bitter, but pecan butter is deliciously sweet. Vitamin E, found in walnuts, is a powerful antioxidant that helps to protect against heart disease. All nuts are rich in B complex vitamins, potassium, magnesium, calcium, phosphorus and iron.

**FRESH IDEA – SPICY PEANUT BUTTER**
This is a tasty peanut butter with chilli and lime that is so much better than any bought versions. Place into a blender 90g/3½oz/scant 1 cup peanuts, ½ small red

chilli, seeded and finely chopped, the juice of 1 lime and 5ml/1 tsp soy sauce. Process until smooth. Add coconut milk to create a dip consistency, and serve with a selection of crunchy crudités.

Made from ground raw sesame seeds and spiced with garlic and lemon juice, this sauce makes a delicious dip served with crudités. Thinned with water, it makes a tasty salad dressing.

# TAHINI DIP

**1** Put the tahini and garlic in a food processor or bowl and mix together well. Stir in the lemon juice, cumin, ground coriander and curry powder.

**2** Slowly add the water to the tahini, beating all the time. The mixture will thicken, then become thin. Season with cayenne pepper.

**3** Serve in a shallow bowl. Drizzle over the oil and sprinkle with the other garnishes.

**COOK'S TIP** Sesame seeds are a rich source of calcium and have cancer-fighting properties. Be sure to buy the tahini made by pressing raw organic sesame seeds as opposed to those processed using toasted seeds.

### FRESH IDEA – SPROUTED HUMMUS

Process 200g/7oz sprouted chickpeas in a food processor to a fine purée. Add 1¹/₂ cloves garlic, the juice of ¹/₂ lemon and 15–30ml/1–2 tbsp tahini. Add a little water

and process to a fine paste. Try using a mixture of other sprouts, for example soybean, aduki or mung beans. These are lower in fat, but higher in carbohydrate; happily all sprouting seeds are rich in vitamins C and E.

Serves 4–6

### INGREDIENTS

150–175g/5–6oz/²/₃–³/₄ cup tahini

3 garlic cloves, finely chopped

juice of 1 lemon

1.5ml/¹/₄ tsp ground cumin

small pinch of ground coriander

small pinch of curry powder

50–120ml/¹/₂–4fl oz/¹/₄–¹/₂ cup water

cayenne pepper

### For the garnish

15–30ml/1–2 tbsp extra virgin olive oil

chopped fresh coriander (cilantro) leaves or parsley

a few chillies or a hot pepper sauce

### NUTRITIONAL INFORMATION

| Per portion | |
|---|---|
| Energy | 193Kcal/808kJ |
| Protein | 110g |
| Carbohydrate | 19g |
| of which sugars | 1g |
| Fat | 9g |
| of which saturates | 1g |
| Cholesterol | 0mg |
| Calcium | 124mg |
| Fibre | 5.3g |
| Sodium | 7mg |

This filling and tasty breakfast can be varied to suit your mood and the available seasonal ingredients. Served with fresh natural yogurt, this muesli is the perfect way to start your day.

# FRESH AND FRUITY MUESLI

**Serves 1**

### INGREDIENTS

1 pear, cored and chopped

1 apple, cored and chopped

1–2 plums, stoned (pitted) and chopped

30–60ml/2–4 tbsp natural (plain) yogurt

30–60ml/2–4 tbsp grain flakes, such as barley, rye or rolled oats

15ml/1 tbsp ground nuts and/or seeds

15ml/1 tbsp raisins

15ml/1 tbsp clear honey (optional)

**1** Place the chopped fruit in a bowl and top with the yogurt then the grain flakes, nuts and raisins. Drizzle the honey over, if using.

**COOK'S TIP** If you prefer the grain flakes to be soft rather than crunchy, try soaking them overnight in apple or orange juice or in a few tablespoons of water. Vary the fruit according to season. In summer and autumn, use fresh soft fruit such as raspberries, strawberries, blackberries and blueberries. In winter and spring, make the most of tropical fruits such as pineapples, papayas, bananas, mangoes and kiwis.

### FRESH IDEA – MAKING YOGURT

It is easy to make yogurt at home – simply use live yogurt as a starter and ensure that it is as fresh as possible. Pour 600ml/1 pint/2½ cups milk into a pan and bring to the boil. Remove from the heat and cool to 32–40°C/90–105°F. Whisk in 15–30ml/1–2 tbsp live yogurt, then pour into a vacuum flask to keep it warm.

Leave for 10–12 hours until set. The yogurt can be kept in the refrigerator for 4–5 days. Once you have made the first batch, you can reserve some of it as the starter to be a culture for the next batch.

### NUTRITIONAL INFORMATION

Per portion

| | |
|---|---|
| Energy | 456Kcal/1926kJ |
| Protein | 11g |
| Carbohydrate | 82g |
| of which sugars | 60g |
| Fat | 12g |
| of which saturates | 0.1g |
| Cholesterol | 0.5mg |
| Calcium | 174mg |
| Fibre | 9.5g |
| Sodium | 67mg |

This refreshingly sweet and fragrant salad looks colourful and tastes good. Adding the lemon juice will help the grated carrot, apple and ginger to keep their natural brightness.

# GRATED CARROT AND APPLE SALAD

**1** In a large bowl, mix together the carrots, apples, ginger, lemon juice or cider apple vinegar and honey.

**2** Place in a small bowl and press down, then tip out on to a plate to make a neat "castle". Top this with the alfalfa and sprinkle with sesame seeds to serve.

**COOK'S TIP** Try this with pears instead of apples, combined with grated courgette (zucchini) instead of the carrots. This cooling choice will give extra vitamin C, and will be lower in sugars too.

**FRESH IDEA – FRUIT AND NUT COLESLAW**
Try this crunchy variation. Finely shred 225g/8oz white cabbage, coarsely grate 1 carrot and place both in a large mixing bowl. Roughly chop 175g/6oz/¾ cup ready-to-eat dried apricots, 50g/2oz/½ cup walnuts, and 50g/2oz/½ cup hazelnuts. Stir them into the cabbage and carrots with 115g/4oz/1 cup raisins and 30ml/ 2 tbsp chopped fresh parsley or chives. In a separate

bowl, mix together 105ml/ 7 tbsp low-fat mayonnaise and 75ml/5 tbsp low-fat natural (plain) yogurt, and season to taste. Add to the coleslaw mixture. Cover and chill for at least 30 minutes before serving.

Serves 1

**INGREDIENTS**

90g/3½oz carrots, peeled and coarsely grated

2 desert apples, coarsely grated

2.5cm/1in piece fresh root ginger, peeled and finely grated

juice of ½ lemon or 15ml/1 tbsp cider apple vinegar

5ml/1 tsp clear honey

small handful alfalfa or other beansprouts

5ml/1 tsp sesame seeds, to serve (optional)

**NUTRITIONAL INFORMATION**

Per portion
| | |
|---|---|
| Energy | 194Kcal/818kJ |
| Protein | 3g |
| Carbohydrate | 41g |
| of which sugars | 39g |
| Fat | 3g |
| of which saturates | 0g |
| Cholesterol | 0mg |
| Calcium | 70mg |
| Fibre | 6.6g |
| Sodium | 36mg |

This satisfying salad has contrasting colours, textures and flavours. The creamy nut dressing, which is full of protein and nutrients, transforms any salad into a wholesome meal.

# SPROUT SALAD WITH CASHEW CREAM DRESSING

Serves 1–2

## INGREDIENTS

130g/4½oz cashew nuts

1 red (bell) pepper, seeded and chopped

90g/3½oz mung bean/aduki bean or chickpea sprouts

½ small cucumber, chopped

juice of ½ lemon

small bunch fresh parsley, coriander (cilantro) or basil, finely chopped

5ml/1 tsp sesame, sunflower or pumpkin seeds

**1** Soak the cashew nuts in 90ml/3½oz/6 tbsp for a few hours, preferably overnight, until plump.

**2** Process the nuts with their soaking water in a food processor until you have a smooth sauce. Add more water if necessary.

**3** Place the pepper, sprouts, cucumber and lemon juice in a bowl and toss together. Serve with the cashew cream scattered with the herbs and seeds.

**COOK'S TIPS** The cashew cream makes a smooth dressing for many different salads or can be used as a sauce. Cashews are rich in monounsaturated fatty acids, as found in the Mediterranean diet, and are favoured for their heart-protecting and anti-cancer properties.

There are all kinds of sprouts, and beansprouts are one of the most readily available commercially. Rinse in cold water before using in salads, juices and other recipes. If you can, choose fresh, crisp sprouts with the seed or bean still attached. Avoid any that are slimy or appear musty. Sprouts are best eaten on the day they are bought, but, if fresh, they will keep for 2–3 days wrapped in a plastic bag in the refrigerator .

## NUTRITIONAL INFORMATION

Per portion
Energy    352Kcal/1459kJ
Protein                    12g
Carbohydrate          18g
 of which sugars     10g
Fat                          26g
 of which saturates   5g
Cholesterol             0mg
Calcium                 78mg
Fibre                      4.7g
Sodium                  19mg.

# INDEX

This refreshingly sweet and fragrant salad looks colourful and tastes good. Adding the lemon juice will help the grated carrot, apple and ginger to keep their natural brightness.

# GRATED CARROT AND APPLE SALAD

**1** In a large bowl, mix together the carrots, apples, ginger, lemon juice or cider apple vinegar and honey.

**2** Place in a small bowl and press down, then tip out on to a plate to make a neat "castle". Top this with the alfalfa and sprinkle with sesame seeds to serve.

**COOK'S TIP** Try this with pears instead of apples, combined with grated courgette (zucchini) instead of the carrots. This cooling choice will give extra vitamin C, and will be lower in sugars too.

**FRESH IDEA – FRUIT AND NUT COLESLAW**
Try this crunchy variation. Finely shred 225g/8oz white cabbage, coarsely grate 1 carrot and place both in a large mixing bowl. Roughly chop 175g/6oz/¾ cup ready-to-eat dried apricots, 50g/2oz/½ cup walnuts, and 50g/2oz/½ cup hazelnuts. Stir them into the cabbage and carrots with 115g/4oz/1 cup raisins and 30ml/ 2 tbsp chopped fresh parsley or chives. In a separate

bowl, mix together 105ml/ 7 tbsp low-fat mayonnaise and 75ml/5 tbsp low-fat natural (plain) yogurt, and season to taste. Add to the coleslaw mixture. Cover and chill for at least 30 minutes before serving.

Serves 1

**INGREDIENTS**

90g/3½oz carrots, peeled and coarsely grated

2 desert apples, coarsely grated

2.5cm/1in piece fresh root ginger, peeled and finely grated

juice of ½ lemon or 15ml/1 tbsp cider apple vinegar

5ml/1 tsp clear honey

small handful alfalfa or other beansprouts

5ml/1 tsp sesame seeds, to serve (optional)

**NUTRITIONAL INFORMATION**

| Per portion | |
| --- | --- |
| Energy | 194Kcal/818kJ |
| Protein | 3g |
| Carbohydrate | 41g |
| of which sugars | 39g |
| Fat | 3g |
| of which saturates | 0g |
| Cholesterol | 0mg |
| Calcium | 70mg |
| Fibre | 6.6g |
| Sodium | 36mg |

This satisfying salad has contrasting colours, textures and flavours. The creamy nut dressing, which is full of protein and nutrients, transforms any salad into a wholesome meal.

# SPROUT SALAD WITH CASHEW CREAM DRESSING

Serves 1–2

**INGREDIENTS**

130g/4½oz cashew nuts

1 red (bell) pepper, seeded and chopped

90g/3½oz mung bean/aduki bean or chickpea sprouts

½ small cucumber, chopped

juice of ½ lemon

small bunch fresh parsley, coriander (cilantro) or basil, finely chopped

5ml/1 tsp sesame, sunflower or pumpkin seeds

**1** Soak the cashew nuts in 90ml/3½oz/6 tbsp for a few hours, preferably overnight, until plump.

**2** Process the nuts with their soaking water in a food processor until you have a smooth sauce. Add more water if necessary.

**3** Place the pepper, sprouts, cucumber and lemon juice in a bowl and toss together. Serve with the cashew cream scattered with the herbs and seeds.

**COOK'S TIPS** The cashew cream makes a smooth dressing for many different salads or can be used as a sauce. Cashews are rich in monounsaturated fatty acids, as found in the Mediterranean diet, and are favoured for their heart-protecting and anti-cancer properties.

There are all kinds of sprouts, and beansprouts are one of the most readily available commercially. Rinse in cold water before using in salads, juices and other recipes. If you can, choose fresh, crisp sprouts with the seed or bean still attached. Avoid any that are slimy or appear musty. Sprouts are best eaten on the day they are bought, but, if fresh, they will keep for 2–3 days wrapped in a plastic bag in the refrigerator .

## NUTRITIONAL INFORMATION

Per portion
| | |
|---|---|
| Energy | 352Kcal/1459kJ |
| Protein | 12g |
| Carbohydrate | 18g |
| of which sugars | 10g |
| Fat | 26g |
| of which saturates | 5g |
| Cholesterol | 0mg |
| Calcium | 78mg |
| Fibre | 4.7g |
| Sodium | 19mg. |